AF413383

A Place to Call Home

Enla Daniel

DEDICATION

To my son, the light of my life, my unwavering supporter and inspiration. Your love, encouragement and belief in my dreams fueled the journey of these tales. As you've stood by me, may these stories stand as a testament to our bond, filled with gratitude for the strength you've added to every chapter of my life.

ABOUT THE AUTHOR

Enla is a compassionate individual who thrives on helping others. Born and raised in the vibrant Tobago of Trinidad and Tobago, a land renowned for its stunning beaches and thriving tourism, Enla has always been surrounded by natural beauty. She holds a degree in business and initially built her career in the financial sector, gaining valuable experience and insights. However, her true calling emerged when she transitioned to the healthcare industry, where she discovered her niche and profoundly impacted people's lives. Enla has a special affinity for the elderly, particularly those struggling to find their place in society, and she works tirelessly to make a difference in their lives.

From a young age, Enla developed a deep passion for writing, a skill that was recognized early on when she was a runner-up in a non-profit slogan competition. This passion, coupled with her inspiration from young readers, has led her to refine her talents and focus on writing for children. Now residing in New Jersey with her child, Enla continues to be an active and engaged member of her community. She hopes that this book will not only entertain but also resonate with its readers, as much as she has enjoyed creating it.

Mary loves animals. She has a beautiful black and white Border Collie named Jenny. Jenny has given birth to the four most beautiful puppies. Mary has been caring for the puppies for the past seven months, but looking after Jenny and her pups is no easy task. It's like having four little bosses, each with their own demands.

For this reason, Mary decides to give the puppies up for adoption. Mary names each of the puppies according to their personalities, and she wants to give them to families that match their unique distinctions. Each family will love them just like they deserve to be loved.

First, there is Rover, the tallest of the bunch. She is frisky, happy, and active, always bouncing around and playing with her siblings. When they are tired of playing, Rover jumps at the flies that come into the house. She rolls around and plays with herself, chasing after her own tail. Rover has lots of energy.

A mother and father come to adopt Rover. They gift her to their eight-year-old twin boys, Josh and Jim. The boys are thrilled with their birthday present! They cuddle Rover and play with him in the backyard. Rover loves every minute of it! They love Rover, and Rover loves them too.

It's a beautiful day! The whole family goes to the park for a walk. They take Rover along with them. They have a lot of fun playing games together and eating their snacks. As they leave the park, Rover's tail wags with excitement as he takes in all the sights and sounds. Suddenly, with a burst of energy, he darts toward a nearby bush under a huge oak tree. Rover stops there and begins sniffing around.

All of a sudden, Rover bends his head down on the
ground, and when he lifts his head, the family is
surprised to see him holding a watch in his mouth.
"Mom, Rover found a gold watch!" Josh shouts.
The mother looks at it and says, "It looks very
expensive! We must take it to the police station. It
could belong to someone who is desperately searching
for it."

"It looks very expensive!"
"Mom, Rover found a gold watch!"

The family takes off toward the police station. As they arrive, a young policeman greets them at the front. Josh and Jim bravely step forward and tell the police officer what has happened. The police officer smiles and praises them for being such good boys. He is impressed with the boys' honesty and for doing the right thing. "Good job, young men!" says the policeman, patting Josh and Jim on the back. "It's people like you who make this world a better place."

POLICE
POLICE
"Good job,
young men!"

The officer tells the parents that a woman has reported losing her gold watch at the park. The parents are very proud of their boys and Rover. They decide to reward them for their good deed. On their way back home, the dad buys ice cream for the kids and dog treats for Rover. Josh and Jim are pleased that they are able to help, and Rover is just happy to be along for the ride.

ICE CREAM SHOP
"Good job, young men!"
Sale
ICE
CREAM

Lucky is Mary's smallest puppy. Despite her small size,
she is calm and charming. She looks cute whenever
she mingles with her other siblings. She always plays
safe and quietly.

Chrissie, a twelve-year-old girl, and her family love dogs. They recently lost their dog due to old age. When they see the adoption sign, the family goes to see the puppies at Mary's home. Chrissie falls in love with Lucky, so her parents adopt her. Lucky finds her new home.

Every evening, Chrissie takes Lucky out for a walk
around the neighborhood. They make many friends in
the area. On the main street, two children often run
down to pet Lucky. Sometimes, a couple stops and pats
Lucky's head. Lucky gets a lot of attention, and she
enjoys the daily walks with Chrissie.

During their walk, Chrissie and Lucky always cross a large house. There, they meet an old lady on her front porch sitting in a rocking chair. She sits outside in the evenings, holding her small poodle named Tiffany. Lucky quickly wins her over with her charming personality, and over time, Lucky and Chrissie become friends with the old lady and Tiffany. The four of them continue to meet in the evening.

One day, Lucky notices something strange. She barks to let Chrissie know that there is no one at the front porch. Chrissie thinks the old woman is busy, so the two of them continue walking. The next day, the same thing happens, but Chrissie ignores it.

On the third day, there is no sign of the old woman or Tiffany; Lucky begins to bark loudly. She runs toward the front porch, and Chrissie follows behind her. When Lucky refuses to leave and continues barking, Chrissie rings the doorbell to ask about the old woman.

A maid answers the door. Chrissie asks for the old
lady, and the maid informs her that she is sick and on
bed rest. Chrissie asks if she can see the old woman
with Lucky. The maid agrees and kindly allows them
into the house to visit the old woman. While in the
room, Lucky raises her paw to the old lady,
greeting her.

Lucky has missed both her friends – the old lady and Tiffany. Chrissie and Lucky visit the old woman every day inside her house until she gets better. The four of them have eventually become lifelong friends.

Holly is the most exciting, mischievous, and amusing of all of Mary's four puppies. She is extremely good-looking, with a snowy white fur coat and black markings around her ears. What makes her stand out from all of the puppies are her eyes, which are a beautiful shade of blue. She likes to play and roll around and mingle with her other siblings.

Mary has a friend called Peter. He, too, loves animals, especially dogs. He has a beautiful Golden Retriever named Happy. Jenny and Happy often go on playdates. When Peter finds out that Mary is putting her puppies up for adoption, he shows up to get Holly.

Happy is full of life and excitement. He is fond of playing games. Holly and Happy play many games together. Peter likes driving them around in his car, and they adore it as they gaze out the window. He loves taking them to the beach. It becomes their favorite place. Both dogs enjoy each other's company. The three of them make a perfect family.

Haley is the last of Mary's puppies. Out of the four, he is the only male, and he is the apple of her eye. He is taller than Holly and Lucky but slightly shorter than Rover. Mary loves him because he is a watchdog. He is always barking, and he is very clever.

Mary wants a suitable home for Haley. It is hard finding the perfect match for him. She refuses many people before she finds the right family. An old couple comes to see her dogs because they want a watchdog for their farm animals. Mary knows at that moment that she has found the right place for Haley at last.

The Powell family has a huge farm with many animals. Haley seems to get his way there; he is the man in charge. He walks around to check that all the animals are safe. He loves being in the fields. He loves sitting with the old couple after his walks.

Haley makes many friends at the farm. He loves playing with Blaze and Pearl, the farm horses. He enjoys taking Pixie, Maxie, and Roxie, the pigs, inside their pen. He has fun watching over Mia and Cassey, the farm cows. He loves the animals, and they adore him too. They are all best friends. This is Haley's ideal life.

When all the puppies are adopted by new families,
Mary becomes very sad. She knows she couldn't care
for them alone. All she wants is to make sure they are
all happy, and she does, but she still misses them.
Jenny misses her puppies too. They often meet with
Peter, Holly, and Happy.

Amazingly, Mary wakes up one day and goes downstairs. There she receives a huge surprise. Jenny is playing with all her puppies again. Happy is with them. Chrissie, Peter, the Powells, Jim, Josh, and their parents are all there too. They have come to celebrate Mary's birthday, which was planned by Peter, who knows how much Mary misses the puppies.

Seeing the puppies so happy, the families decide to meet every month. They take turns to host. They meet every year on Mary's birthday. The Powells have a BBQ party every few months, which everyone enjoys. Peter takes the entire group to the beach, and they all have fun. Chrissie graduates middle school and calls everyone to celebrate at the park. Jim and Josh have a pool party at their place every summer. They all form a close bond and enjoy each other's company. They could not have been happier. Little do Mary and Jenny know these new friends would become their family.

HAPPY BIRTHDAY

A Place to Call Home

ABOUT THE BOOK

Witness a heartwarming journey with Mary and her four adorable puppies as they search for their perfect homes. Each puppy possesses a unique personality, from the adventurous Scout to the gentle Bella, making the story a delightful read for children.

As Mary lovingly nurtures her furry friends, young readers will discover the importance of friendship, kindness, and the joy of finding one's place in the world. The enchanting tale unfolds with vibrant illustrations that bring the characters to life, capturing the imagination of children and adults alike.

Join the excitement as the puppies explore the world, encounter new friends, and face challenges together. Through engaging storytelling and charming illustrations, "A Place To Call Home" entertains and imparts valuable lessons about love, acceptance, and the true meaning of family. This heartening children's book is sure to become a cherished favorite, inviting readers to dream and discover the magic of finding their place to call home.

Enla Daniel